Bayeux

a town of artistic and architectural interest

TEXT
JACQUES BILLY

PHOTOGRAPHS
HERVÉ CHAMPOLLION

Above
The R. Aure flows peacefully through the district that was once home to dyers. On the right, in the background, is the Crocqueville Mill.

Summary

TRANSLATED BY ANGELA MOYON

ÉDITIONS OUEST-FRANCE

"IT is highly unusual to see a town peaceably nestling round its cathedral without any factory chimneys in among the bellcotes, stretching out its arms in gentle provincial boredom of a type that has its own charm and leaves long hours free for daydreaming. We have often said that Time no longer exists except in the gilded bronze of old timepieces. Yet Time does exist; we have found it in Bayeux, a town which is very well-preserved for its age. How strange it is to think that, when so many solidly-built constructions have collapsed, this fragile strip of cloth has survived intact the passing centuries, revolutions and disasters of every kind!"

(Théophile Gautier, *Quand on voyage*, 1865.)

From Celtic Origins to Norman Domination

Bayeux was already an important town before the Christian era, with a flourishing trade in produce from the surrounding countryside and nearby sea. At the gateway to the town, on Mount Phaunus in the heart of an oak forest (the Celtic word for oaks is "*Casses*"), druids held ceremonies in honour of Belus, the Sun God. It is said that the association of these two words produced the name "Belocasses" (now "Bajocasses") which is used for the people of Bayeux.

Mount Phaunus is thought to have been the seat of various major druid communities whose prestige spread far beyond the immediate vicinity. This is evident in the praise given by Ausonius, preceptor to Emperor Gratian, to one of their descendents, Patera, a poet initiated into the rites surrounding the worship of Apollo.

Tu baiocassi stirpe druidarum satus
Si fama fallit fidem
Beleni sacratum ducis e templo genus". "Born of a line of druids from Bayeux / If what is said is not designed to mislead / Yours is a sacred lineage drawn from the temple of Belenus". (This text was quoted by Father Jean Marie in *Bayeux, ville d'art*).

Mill, rue de Nesmond. ▶

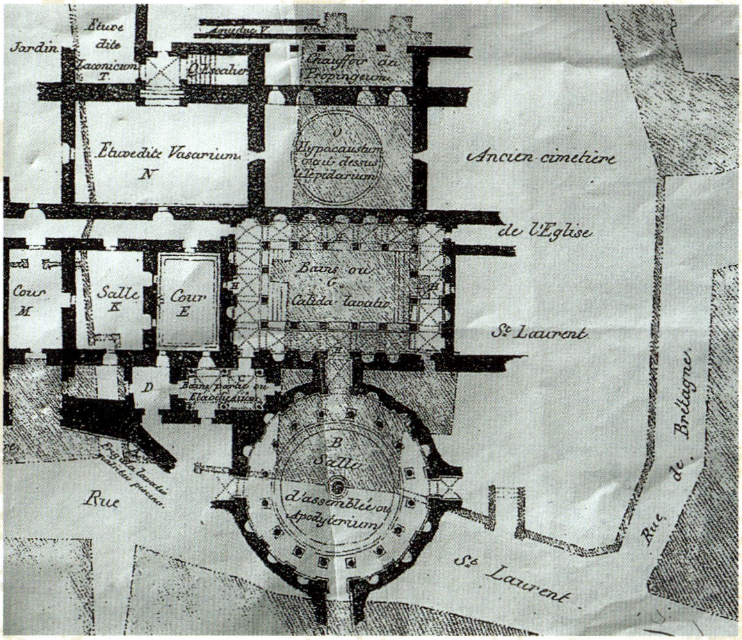

◀ *Baths.*

Situated at the foot of the sacred hill, in the dip formed by the Aure Valley (the name comes from the Celtic "*ar*" meaning "river"), the town was already fairly important at the beginning of the Christian era, as is evident from the fact that the Bajocasses sent a large contingent of warriors to support Vercingetorix at the Battle of Alesia.

The subsequent Roman occupation was initially marked by the building of a military encampment on the left bank of the R. Aure, round the area now known as Place du Château, while the town itself was sited further north.

Bayeux was a Roman town on the major road leading to Cherbourg and, for some time, it was known as Augustodurum, literally "citadel of Augustus", a privilege reserved for only a small number of towns in the Empire. After the division of Gaul into seven administrative regions, Bayeux became the capital of one of them with the rank of municipality. It then had a forum, basilica and baths. The remains of this Roman town have been discovered in the Saint-Laurent District and in Rue Laitière.

Druidism was replaced by the polytheistic religions of the Romans.

Towards the end of the 3rd century, Bayeux reached its heyday as an imperial town. However, the Roman Empire was under threat from all quarters. In 276 and again in

▼ *In the centre of Place du Général-de-Gaulle (formerly Place du Château), the statue of Poppa stands majestically above the fountain.*

REMAINS OF GALLO-ROMAN BAYEUX

Bayeux, a major town during Gallo-Roman times, still has a large number of remains in various places within today's urban community. In Rue Saint-Laurent, there are the remains of the baths; the theatre and forum used to stand nearby. The archaeological digs undertaken around the cathedral built on the site of a temple dedicated to a Gallo-Roman god revealed columns and sculptures dating from the Dark Ages. More baths were found in Rue Laitière and, in 1994, a large Gallo-Roman lime kiln was discovered near the western exit from the town.

Walls used to encircle the *castrum* situated to the west and it was here that the castle was built. It was destroyed in 1773 on the eve of the French Revolution, razed to the ground in 1804 and the site is now occupied by the Place Général-de-Gaulle. Numerous remains of the town walls have survived to the present day.

Gallo-Roman hypocaust discovered in Rue Laitière. ▲

The statue of Poppa. ▶

368 A.D, the Saxons ransacked and set fire to the town then occupied the entire region. Gregory of Tours held discussions with the Saxons of Bayeux in 578 A.D and, in 853 A.D, Charles the Bald sent envoys to the Cherbourg Peninsula, Bessin area and Otlinga Saxonia, an indication that the Saxon influence was long-lasting. It was even evident in the language.

After 511 A.D, the town passed into the hands of the kings of the Franks. It became a provostry c. 560 A.D and it was here that the provincial governor meted out justice. Coins were minted bearing the inscription "*bajocas*".

The period of peace which preceded the arrival of the Normans was, like the conversion of Clovis, to promote the spread of Christianity in the Bayeux region. The early days were difficult. In the 4th century, the town still had only a small number of Christian families and they kept alive memories of St. Floxel who had been martyred by the Romans in the previous century. Mount Phaunus was undoubtedly one of the early places of worship, as shown by the remains of a baptistery discovered by Arcisse de Caumont (he was born in Bayeux in 1802), but during the days of the first bishops Christians also gathered on the spot where the cathedral was later built. The very first bishop was St. Exupère (4th century). He was succeeded by St. Loup *c.* 440 A.D, St. Manvieu in 470, St. Contest c. 480-510 A.D, and St. Vigor in 511. They were venerated by the Christians and their names were later given to the parishes around Bayeux.

The Arrival of the Normans

The first Viking invasions in this region took place in 844 A.D Two years later, Bayeux was laid to waste by furious hordes of Bretons. In 848 A.D, the town was again ransacked by the Normans who also killed Bishop Baltfride. A period of peace followed but, in 890, Rollo captured Bayeux and the conquerors brutally murdered any townspeople caught with weapons in their hands. The cruel conqueror, though, fell in love with the beautiful Poppa, daughter of Count Bérenger, the unfortunate defender of the town. Rollo took her as his wife *more danico* (i.e. in the Danish manner) and they had a son, William Longsword, in 905 A.D who succeeded Rollo as Duke of Normandy in 930. His great-grandson was William the Conqueror.

It was, then, the marriage of a Viking chieftain and a woman from Bayeux that produced the glorious dynasty of the Dukes of Normandy who were also, it should be remembered, Kings of England for one hundred and thirty-eight years from 1066, the year in which William was crowned in London on Christmas Day, to 1204, the year in which King John was defeated at Château-Gaillard. Thereafter Normandy was annexed to France and this put an end to the ascendancy of Bayeux and its role as a cultural centre where the Saxon language was spoken for many years. After being the second most important town in Normandy, it was downgraded in 1258 to the rank of lieutenancy general dependant on the bailiwick of Caen.

▲ *The Romanesque crypt has three aisles and six spans with ribbed vaulting.*

The Cathedral

The cathedral stands on the site of a Gallo-Roman temple. Several timber churches were built in the early centuries of Christianity before the construction of a stone church in the

◄ *One of the angel musicians in the crypt, at the top of a capital decorated with acanthus leaves.*

11th century under the authority of the Bishop of Bayeux, Odo of Conteville, William the Conqueror's half-brother. The new church was consecrated amid much pomp on 14th July 1077, in the presence of the Duke of Normandy and the Bishops of York and Canterbury. It was probably on this occasion that the *Bayeux Tapestry,* or "Queen Matilda's Tapestry", or the "Tale of the Conquest", was exhibited for the first time; it was hung up in the nave.

A few sections of the original cathedral, having escaped fire damage in 1105 during Henry I Beauclerc's siege of Bayeux and again in 1160, can still be seen in the building today, in particular the Romanesque crypt uncovered in 1412 and the piers on the west front.

The exterior shows a determination to achieve originality and sculptural magnificence. The towers, which are 73 metres - 237 ft. high, consist of ten storeys topped by spires decorated at

The façade of the cathedral. ▶

A general view of the cathedral. ▶

the base with four bellturrets. They are striking for their grace and sense of upwards movement. The west front was seriously damaged during the Wars of Religion but the conflict spared the tympana on the side doors (Passion and Last Judgement Portals). The doors in the central entrance are decorated with fleurs-de-lys and two-headed eagles which may be the old coat-of-arms of Bayeux.

It is the doorway in the south transept opposite the Deanery (*hôtel du Doyen*) that is the most interesting. The carvings on the tympanum depict the martyrdom of St. Thomas à Becket.

The central tower dates from the late 15th century. On 25th March 1499, when he took possession of the cathedral, Monsignor de Prie celebrated Mass at the top of the tower then blessed the awestruck crowd of thousands below. The dome at the very top posed many problems because of the weakness of the supports - one of the pillars in the transept crossing threatened to collapse. It was a railway engineer, Eugène Flachat, who found a daring technical solution and who, in 1858, ensured that the building as a whole would withstand the passage of time. Viollet-le-Duc took advantage of this work to give the first span in the nave back its Romanesque style.

The interior gives an impression of majesty. The nave is 23 metres - 75 ft. high, and 11.50 metres - 37 ft. high, and is built in a combination of Romanesque and Gothic styles. The chancel has three storeys, the last one being the clerestory above the triforium consisting of gemel windows. The decoration of the particularly fine altar by Alfred Caffieri dates from 1771. The elegantly-carved choirstalls were made by a cabinetmaker from Caen, Jacques Lefèvre; they date from the Renaissance. Beneath the pavement in the ambulatory leading to nine apsidal chapels are the tombs of bishops. The south crossing in the transept is decorated with 15th century murals depicting the murder of St. Thomas à Becket. Each of the aisles (they were built in 1165) has

▲ ***A general view of the nave with its Romanesque lower section and Gothic upper section.***

FRESCOES IN THE CHAPELS IN THE SOUTH TRANSEPT

Situated in the south transept, the 15th century frescoes are striking for their originality, their beauty and their condition.
The ones on the left depict the Holy Trinity in the topmost section. The Holy Spirit is illustrated as a dove rather strangely flanked by God in Majesty and Christ on the Cross. In the background, beneath a star-studded sky, is a naive illustration of Bayeux cathedral. The lower section depicts the Archangel Gabriel and the Annunciation of the Virgin Mary.
On the right, the upper section dates from the 19th century; it depicts the murder of Thomas à Becket, the subject already featured on the tympanum of the south door. Below it are two different subjects in frescoes dating from the 15th century.
On the upper level is the Crucifixion and on the lower section the miracles worked by St. Nicholas i.e. the children slaughtered by the butcher and ressuscitated in his salting room, the alms given to a penniless father to save his daughter from prostitution, the child saved from a fire, and the pilgrimage to the Holy Land during which the saint was miraculously spared by a storm.
The fresco is surrounded by a quatrefoil motif which is a repetition of the motif seen in the upper section of the Romanesque part of the nave.

one chapel. The chapter house extends beyond the north wall. Built in the 13th century, it was heightened in the following century. A fresco of the Virgin Mary with cherubim and angels playing the psaltery decorates the north wall. In the middle of the glazed brick pavement is the labyrinth, a feature rarely seen in France.

The cathedral has had a succession of organs. One was destroyed in 1562 by the Protestants. The second one was inaugurated in 1596 and was built by Jacques Lefèvre who had carved the choirstalls and by Jean d'Arguillières. The great organ at the end of the church was installed in 1644-1647. In 1862, Cavaillé-Coll increased the number of stops. This organ is of such an outstandingly high quality that it is often used by famous organists for public concerts.

The other religious buildings were

erected in several stages to the north and east and these buildings, which have now been reconstructed, flank the square on which stands the Tree of Liberty. All that remains of the cloisters which once lay next to the cathedral are the Romanesque arches that can be seen in the courtyard of the Baron-Gérard Museum next to the Town Hall. The museum buildings date from various periods.

The Town in the Middle Ages

In those days, Bayeux was a typical mediaeval town lying in the shadow of its cathedral. Every morning, the bells of the mother church and some twenty or more parish churches woke the townspeople sleeping safe and snug within the town walls flanked by a moat and dotted with eighteen defensive towers of which a few traces have survived to the present time. The castle was in the north-west corner, within the walls but separated from the town itself by another high wall. The community was not only under threat of

▲ *The superb Romanesque arches in the nave, decorated with a range of different motifs. In the squinches are carvings of sacred figures and animals drawn from a fantasy world.*

◄ *The nave. The bishop blessing one of the squinches.*

TIMBERED HOUSES

Four of them have been spared by fire and the passage of time and are still there, like the cathedral, to give some idea of what the mediaeval town used to look like.

Firstly, there is the so-called Adam and Eve House (*maison d'Adam et Eve*) on whose frontage are wooden statuettes representing characters from the Old and New Testaments. Then, at the corner of Rue des Cuisiniers and Rue de Saint-Martin, there are two semi-detached houses dating from the reign of Charles VII. They were originally shops but were later turned into an inn and are now the seat of the "Bayeux Accueil" tourist authority. Further up Rue Saint-Martin is another timbered house dating from the 14th century. The most impressive of them all, however, is undoubtedly the Grand Hôtel d'Argouges whose frontage is covered in statuettes of the Virgin Mary and the saints. In the inner courtyard is a polygonal Renaissance tower. In April 1532, François I spent four days in this superb mansion.

The frontage of the Grand Hôtel d'Argouges. ▼

▲ *Three of the naive woodcarvings decorating the beams on the ground floor that support the corbelling on the Adam and Eve House: The Child King symbolising the Child Jesus.*

invasion; there was the risk of epidemics and fire which spread quickly between the timbered houses lining the narrow alleyways with names evocative of the crafts and trades of days long gone.

The castle stood on the site now occupied by Place Général-de-Gaulle. It was razed to the ground in the late 18th century but the King's market on Place Saint-Patrice has retained its original purpose. The square was also the

▲ *Three of the naive woodcarvings decorating the beams on the ground floor that support the corbelling on the Adam and Eve House: St. Michael slaying the dragon.*

scene of public executions - the condemned were burnt at the stake, executed on the block or hung.

Not all the many churches scattered throughout the mediaeval town have disappeared. In the courtyard of the Centre Guillaume-le-Conquérant, there is a former Augustinian chapel dating from the 13th century; it has graceful Gothic vaulting. Saint-Nicolas-des-Courtils stands at the end of a narrow alleyway opening onto Rue Général-de-Dais and is mentioned in a cartulary dating from 1303. It was a collegiate church founded by boatmen and traders and, in the Middle Ages, it was the seat of a brotherhood. All that remains of the old church is one transept with its trefoiled frieze.

ALAIN CHARTIER, THE PATRIOTIC POET, ONE OF BAYEUX' SONS

Alain Chartier was born c. 1385 and died in 1433 and he is one of the best-known of the town's sons. He was secretary to Charles VI, and the author not only of courtly poems including *La Belle Dame sans Mercy* (1424) but also, more importantly, *Quadrilogue invectif* which was written in 1422 during the darkest days of the wars. It is a debate in prose between four allegorical figures in which France exhorts its children (the Knight, the Clergy and the People) to unite in the face of the English invader.

On the front of his birthplace in Rue Saint-Patrice is a plaque in his honour and in honour of his brothers, Jean, Charles VII's historiographer, and Guillaume who was Bishop of Paris.

The poet's statue stands at the entrance to Place Général-de-Gaulle, which used to be known as Place du Château. It is only a few yards from the cathedral.

▲ *Statue of Alain Chartier.*

For Bayeux, the One Hundred Years' War was a time of great misfortune. After bitter fighting, the destruction of the town in 1356 and an initial period of English occupation which ended with the signing of the Treaty of Brétigny, Bayeux was forced to surrender to King Henry II of England in 1417. The monarch, forgetting his promises, then distributed sinecures and property to his vassals. In 1434, the town was in the grip of abject poverty and the townspeople rebelled. It was then that Roland des Talents addressed his complaint to the Duke of Gloucester and Alain Chartier wrote his *Quadrilogue invectif*. On 19th May 1450, after the Battle of Formigny, the town was finally liberated and nine hundred English men-of-arms left, dressed in civilian clothes, some of them accompanied by their Norman wives and children. A century of relative peace followed and the local people took advantage of it to rebuild the town. However, this peace was followed by another period of strife, marked by the Wars of Religion and, later, by the Fronde revolt.

In 1562, the cathedral was ransacked by the Protestants who also massacred the townspeople. The two camps captured and lost the town in turn, pillaging its treasures and the cathedral. It was not until 1590 that the town was re-occupied by Catholic troops led by the Duke de Montpensier. When Henri IV abjured his Protestant faith in 1593, he put an end to this bloody period of history.

Bayeux in the Days of the Great Lords (16th-17th centuries)

▼ Hôtel de Rubercy in Rue Franche. On the upper storey, the mullioned window opens onto a bedchamber with fireplace.

Tower Houses

The townspeople's determination to protect and defend themselves against brigands and, on some occasions, the English, manifested itself during these troubled times in the unusual architecture that can be seen in the old town and its suburbs. The doors and windows are small and there are spiral staircases leading up to watchtowers, sometimes including slit windows. These are the characteristic features of the 16th century buildings that replaced the old timbered houses. We have already mentioned the tower in the courtyard of the mansion known as Grand Hôtel d'Argouges. Other tower houses are equally eye-catching in the narrow streets around the cathedral.

Firstly, there is the Maison de Gilles Buhot at the corner of Rue de la Juridiction and Rue Franche. Its tower has a saddleback roof rising from a façade devoid of ornamentation. Also in Rue Franche is the Hôtel de Rubercy. Its square tower with mullioned windows has a corbelled half-turret on one side. The Hôtel Saint-Manvieu (at no. 13) was named after a 4th century bishop, initially a hermit, who was said to have been born on this spot. Legend has it that he brought a local child back to life.

▼ *The mansion known as the Maison de Gilles Buhot in Rue de la Juridiction at the corner of Rue Franche.*

▲ *The Hôtel du Gouverneur in Rue Bourbesneur (note the square turret containing a spiral staircase that leads up to the room on the upper floor). The mansion now houses the De Gaulle Memorial.*

The Hôtel du Governeur in Rue Bourbesneur is striking for its elegance and a certain majesty. The lower section dates from the 15th century. It has mullioned windows overlooking the courtyard and street. The tower is hexagonal at the base but square at roof level. Adjacent to it is a small square turret. The house gets its name

The Hôtel du Croissant. ▲

from its use, in the 18th century, as the residence of the governor, Mr. Couvert de Coulon. It has belonged to the town council since 1912 and the magnificent building now houses the Mémorial De Gaulle which was opened in 1990.

The Hôtel du Croissant at the end of a narrow alleyway at right angles to Rue Saint-Jean is another fine reminder of the days of the war lords. The "Crescent House" stands proud and tall, with a four-storey tower topped by a saddleback roof and narrow windows that become taller and taller towards the uppermost part of the building. This impressive tower has rooms on all floors. In the street is a coat-of-arms with three stars and a crescent moon, said to be a reminder of the houseowner's participation in the crusades.

Many other old houses in Bayeux still have their towers, including the Manoir de La Cambette in Rue Saint-Loup. Its tower can be seen in the inner courtyard; it contains a spiral staircase that opens onto independant bedrooms. In the Hôtel de Colombiers, the tower is visible from Rue des Ursulines but the façade overlooking Rue Général-de-Dais, which was built in a much later period, is an example of Renaissance architecture. Two rows of slightly projecting windows flanked by pilasters lie to each side of a tall, narrow doorway topped by a triangular pediment.

Buildings from the Reign of Louis XIII
(1610-1643)

A tour of three buildings typical of this period immediately transports visitors back to the days of Louis XIII, the Fronde Revolt and proud noblemen reminiscent of the Three Musketeers. The architecture still expresses a certain military rigour but it has lost the heavy feeling of the tower houses, probably as a result of the widespread influence of the Renaissance.

A fine example of this style can be seen at 18 Rue Général-de-Dais, once the house of the Former Literary Circle. It has an austere façade topped

◄ *Louis XIII mansion.*

by an arrogant, pointed roof. The entrance consists of a door topped by 15th century arching. The same majestic style of roof, this time flanked by a tall chimney with triangular pediments, can be seen in Rue Saint-Patrice, in the Manoir de La Caillerie built in 1647. The magnificent, austere frontage of this manor house is lightened (*left*) by an arch with voussoirs above the carriage entrance. Above the arch is a cornice with separate, rounded pediments. The mansion at 17 Rue de la Maîtrise is a more elegant building. It was purchased in 1642 by Equerry Thomas Morel, Lord of La Carbonnière, who had it rebuilt in the fashionable style of the day. Its most outstanding features, the dormer windows with arched pediments and the tall chimney with triangular pediment, are visible from the street. The staircase with loggia is of Italian inspiration; it has been closed from the outside. The Hôtel Eon de Cely next to the Hôtel Saint-Manvieu in Rue Franche was built during the same period.

The most exceptional reminder of the Renaissance period is the tower on St. Patrick's Church (*église Saint-Patrice*), a composite building on which work began in the 12th century but which was extensively altered in the the Gothic period and again in 1746 when the chancel and transept were rebuilt. The tower has seven floors. It was built from 1548 onwards. The first four floors are square; the last three form a dome, with a tiny top floor. The tower was commissioned by a merchant named Samson, then owner of the manor house opposite the church. The house bears his name.

St. Patrick's Church. ►

La Charité convent. ▲

The Reign of Louis XIV: Religious Buildings take Priority

The long period of peace enjoyed by Bayeux during the reign of this great monarch was not marked by any apparent opulence. The repeated wars in foreign countries and the range of privileges enjoyed by the nobility caused misery and hardship. In reaction against this situation, men of the cloth who came from wealthy families had huge buildings constructed in Bayeux, some of them of a religious nature, others designed for charity work or teaching. Most of them are now used for secular purposes.

The most venerable of all these establishment was the Hospital (*Maison-Dieu*) dating back to the 13th century; it was commissioned by Bishops Guy and Robert des Ablèges. At the beginning of Louis XIV's reign, the buildings were considerably extended and, in 1641, the Augustinian Sisters of Mercy were asked to take over their management from the Austin Canons whose work was widely criticised. St. Catherine de Longpré, who was beatified in 1989 (statue), spent a long time here before setting off for Quebec. The 17th century buildings in Allée des Augustines opposite the entrance to the Centre Guillaume-le-Conquérant (the chapel is open to the public) have been integrated into the general hospital. In 1651, it was the Ursuline Order which extended and refurbished the buildings in Rue Saint-Patrice and, in 1664, they opened a girls' school there. It was closed down in 1792. The municipal secondary school, which later became a senior high school, took over the buildings in 1804.

In 1653, La Charité was set up in Bayeux on Place Saint-Patrice further to royal authorisation in the form of letters patent. It was initially a small institution for young women in distress but, in 1706, Roger de Vigney, the king's prosecutor, who had already lost two children and was desperately unhappy at the irrevocable departure of his only surviving daughter when she entered the convent decided, with his wife, to have a magnificent chapel built with chancel, gallery and sacristy to designs by the great architect from Bayeux, Jacques Moussard. Today, its west front stands in line with Rue Royale, forming the superb backcloth to Place Saint-Patrice. All the buildings are now used for secular purposes.

The hospice is a home for old people, including those with handicaps. It stands at the top of Rue Saint-Jean on the Caen road and dates from 1676. It was set up at the behest of the bishop, Monsignor de Nesmond, a great and generous man of impeccable taste who did not restrict his actions to the building of charitable institutions, often funded out of his own pocket, like this one designed originally for paupers and old people with nowhere else to go. He also commissioned a number of superb buildings in the Classical style which broke away from the more usual towers, pointed roofs and ornate decoration.

The finest example of this is the Grand Seminary in Rue de Nesmond which has also gained a secular purpose and now houses the Centre Guillaume-le-Conquérant. It is here that visitors can see the Bayeux Tapestry. Building work began on the seminary in 1693 on the site of the priory belonging to the Canons of St. Augustine until they left it in 1675. All that remains of the priory is the delightful 13th century chapel. As to the superb seminary building, its most striking feature is its austerity. A wide flight of steps leads from the courtyard up to the entrance protected by a balustrade.

The death of Monsignor de Nesmond in 1715 (the same year as the Sun King), who had finally acquired the nickname the "Bishop of the Trowel", marked the end of an era. Unable to rival Caen as a political and administrative city, the town became a major centre of religious life. Behind the walls of institutions such as the Grand Seminary, premises belonging to brotherhoods, the hospital and the hospice, priests, monks, clerics and nuns prepared for, or lived out, a life in the service of God.

▲ ***Exhibition room of the Bayeux Tapestry.***
Ph. J.Y. Labartette.

▼ ***The Grand Seminary, today the Centre Guillaume-le-Conquérant and home of the Bayeux Tapestry.***
Ph. Bayeux public library.

◀ *The front of the meat market (1784) in Rue Saint-Martin. A door topped by a tympanum decorated with Bayeux' coat-of-arms.*

The 18th century and Urban Expansion

"He who has not lived in the 18th century has not experienced the sweetness of life", wrote Talleyrand.

Major changes were to mark the reigns of Louis XV (1715-1776) and Louis XVI in Bayeux. The town enjoyed industrial and commercial expansion facilitated by the development of popular education. At the same time, a new form of town planning evolved and its effect was heightened still further by the construction of magnificent private mansions.

Economic Development

In 1747, Father Suard opened the first school for underprivileged girls. His initiative coincided with the inauguration of the lace making factory, lace being one of Bayeux' specialities after pottery which has given its name to one of the streets in the town. A short distance upstream from the bridge over the R. Aure which was rebuilt during the reign of Louis XVI is the dyers' district remembered in the Crocquevieille Mill, mill race and old houses, all of which have recently been restored. In the nearby Saint-Laurent District, a wool and cotton mill was set up in 1757. Trade, too, flourished as is obvious in the fine doorway to the meat market in Rue Saint-Martin, dating from 1784 and topped by the town's coat-of-arms.

From the 1770's onwards, when the town council was chaired by Mr. Larcher de La Londe, the town underwent a number of other changes that were to give it a more modern appearance. Insalubrious districts were rendered more healthy places to live, the streets were cobbled, their practicability was improved and a firefighting service was introduced. The first street lights were introduced in 1782.

BAYEUX LACE

It was in the mid 18th century that a lace factory was opened in Bayeux and the town became famous throughout the province for the craft which occupied families during the long winter evenings. Although the factory was eventually closed, the local people never lost their love of lace making and, in 1982, a lace making school was set up.
Bayeux lace is made with bobbins, like the lace from Le Puy and Bruges but unlike Alençon lace which is needlepoint. This being so,

it is incorrect to talk about a "Bayeux stitch". However, there is a Bayeux style, evident in the design of some of the pieces. The finest of them all are displayed in the town's Baron-Gérard Museum but are also the subject of temporary exhibitions in Bayeux and elsewhere.
Lace making is being perpetuated in the town although today the production is mainly restricted to small pieces. The lace makers are trained locally. There are weekly lessons for children of school age, as part of their leisure activities; there are also one-week courses for adults from Bayeux and elsewhere. The training is provided by professional lace makers holding a diploma from the National hand lace academy (*Conservatoire national de la dentelle à la main*) in Le Puy-en-Velay in central France.

▲ *The frontage on the Hôtel de Castelly in Rue Général-de-Dais.*

New Townhouses and the Bishop's Palace

Until the years leading up to the French Revolution, a number of magnificent private mansions were built in the town, so many of them, in fact, that it is impossible to list them all. The most outstanding one is the Hôtel de Castilly in Rue Général-de-Dais which dates from 1747 and was

▲ *The front of the Town Hall (1770) in the same Louis XV style, evident in the top of the windows, the pediment and its highly ornate tympanum.*

▲ *A typical Louis XVI style housefront with balcony and garlands. This is the Hôtel de Bricqueville, a mansion also known as the Hôtel de la Tour du Pin in Rue Général-de-Dais.*

another of Jacques Moussard's designs. Beyond the wrought-iron gates at the end of the courtyard stands the main building flanked by two wings. It is a perfect design, with tall windows and a triangular pediment including a tympanum on which the sculpture has been destroyed. A few yards further on towards Place du Château is the majestic Hôtel de la Tour du Pin, more correctly known as the Hôtel de Bricqueville, decorated with garlands and ribbons in a style typical of the Louis XVI period. It also has a wide balcony above the carriage entrance. The courtyard is inside and opens onto the former town walls. Almost opposite this mansion is a fine Louis XV house (*no. 23*) that is attractive for the austere elegance of its dimensions.

At the corner of Rue de la Juridiction and Rue des Ursulines is the "Bonbonnière", a charming house that is smothered in flowers in the summer months.

In the Bessin area, the lesser nobility and wealthy middle classes took advantage of this period of prosperity to develop a certain way of life and commission the building of fine mansions in the elegant Louis XV style.

Since Bayeux had a number of Law Courts and, moreover, the Upper Council for Normandy was set up in the town in 1771, gentlemen of the robe also built or purchased houses. Their example was then followed by a number of officers commanding the troops whose job it was to protect the coast against attack by the British.

The Bishop did not want to be left out. In 1770, Monsignor de Rochechouart had the Bishop's Palace built, privately funded by his own family. It has become the Town Hall. The superb frontage faces eastwards and overlooks the gardens. It has a ceremonial balcony and a pediment with a graceful tympanum decorated with the coat-of-arms of Bayeux flanked by two nymphs carrying a winged staff and a cornucopia. A huge entrance and a passageway lead to the square on the north side of the cathedral and the small group of buildings from several different historical periods which includes the Baron-Gérard Museum. On the upper floor of the south wing are the magnificent lobby that is now used as for civic receptions and the former courtroom that is now the Council chamber. The end of the building that almost reaches Rue Larcher runs into the attractive 16th century chapel with its elegantly decorated ceiling. The chapel was commissioned by Bishop Louis de Canossa.

The Deanery (*hôtel du Doyen*) dates from the end of the 1730's and was built under the Deanship of Neel de Cristot. It can be found at the end of a

flower-filled courtyard opposite the south wall of the catheral. It now houses the Lace Making School, the Museum of Sacred Art and a number of exhibitions. It stands out in Rue Lambert-Leforestier because of its huge portal dating from 1697 topped by a balustrade.

The town expanded and fine mansions were no longer built solely in old districts. At 14 Rue Royale, the first floor and pediment of the Hôtel de Royville can be seen peeping over

▲ *One of the doors and the lavishly-decorated wall on the bishop's private chapel commissioned in the 16th Century by Bishop Louis de Canossa at the western end of the buildings in the Bishop's Palace overlooking Rue Larcher.*

◄ *The Deanery staircase.*

▲ *The superb decoration on the Maison du Cadran (1798) in Rue Saint-Martin. To the left, at the top, is the sundial; at the bottom, the signs of the zodiac.*

▲ *The Hôtel "de la Du Barry"*

the tall walls. This is a superbly impressive house named after its first owner. In Rue Larcher almost at the corner of Rue de la Nesmond opposite the cathedral is the Hôtel de la du Barry, named after the famous countess who, in fact, only ever spent a few days there. It has an admirable, elegant forepart projecting from the cornice and topped by a pediment with a delicately carved tympanum.

At 36 Rue des Bouchers, slender elegant windows and a forepart with tiers of pilasters and balconies attract attention to the Hôtel Tillard des Acres. At no. 76 in the same street, on the other hand, the style is resolutely Louis XVI in the Hôtel de Langalerie on which the portal is decorated with garlands.

The Maison du Cadran (*Sundial House*) in Rue Saint-Martin was built in 1798 and is one of the most successful examples of late 18th century architecture, with its very tall pilasters and huge wrought-iron balcony created by an ironsmith named Lebreton. Many of these private residences are still furnished in the corresponding delightful period styles.

In the evenings, the superb mansions used to be brilliantly lit for dazzling receptions. In September 1778, after the opening of the army camp in Vaussieux on the outskirts of the town, festivities were held for a whole month in the camp itself where the hospitality was lavish and in the mansions where receptions were attended by high-ranking dignitiaries including the Duke de Broglie and the Duke d'Harcourt, the Prince and Princess Beauvau, and Dumouriez. In 1782, the Countess Du Barry visited her brother-in-law who was C-in-C of the Bayeux Regiment. In 1788, the hospitality culminated in the visit of King Louis XVI who was welcomed on Place Saint-Patrice by the Governor, the Duke d'Harcourt, and by the mayor, Mr. Larcher de La Londe, who presented him with the keys of the town on a silver platter. The street leading from the site of the castle to the square then took the name Rue Royale.

The French Revolution marked the end of opulence and luxurious living for the gentlemen of the robe and the local nobility who had become accustomed to a whirlwind social life, and for the clergy, many of whom were the sons of very wealthy families.

Disturbances during the French Revolution

Bayeux was an eminently aristocratic town but it did not escape unscathed from the torments of the French Revolution.

It seemed, initially at least, as if traditional values would carry the day, with the bishop, Monsignor de Cheylus, being elected mayor in January 1790. He was forced to resign eleven months later. When the Civil Constitution was applied to the clergy in April 1791, his successor, Father Fruchet, took over the position. The struggle between Church and State gradually came into being. Clubs were founded in the Augustinian priory then in the Bishop's Palace. The Reign of Terror was marked by prison sentences passed at the request of the local branch of the Committee of Public Salvation. The former Franciscan convent in Rue Saint-Loup was used as a prison for non-juring priests and, later, as a warehouse for objects that had been officially confiscated. The cathedral was turned into a Temple of Reason and the Supreme Being, and the corresponding festival was an opportunity for a dazzling celebration. It was then that the Trees of Liberty were planted. They were replaced, on 10th Germinal of Year V, by the tree that now stands majestically on the square between the cathedral and the Town Hall. It will be two hundred years old in 1997.

Meanwhile, royalist rebels were increasing their support in the Bessin area. Mr. Jehanne, chairman of the municipal council, opposed General Barbazan's intervention when the army officer besieged the town. Eighteen rebels were executed on 24th Pluviose of Year IV during the period of repression that followed.

Order was not really re-established until after 18th Brumaire. The bishop then regained possession of his cathedral and Bayeux became a sub-prefecture. The lower Courts and Commercial Court were all set up. The town was about to step into the middle-class 19th century.

▲ *The Tree of Liberty, on the square of the same name. In the background, to the left, is the entrance to the Baron-Gérard Museum (the frontage was altered in the 15th century).*

From the French Revolution to the 1940's, Bayeux enjoyed the peaceful existence of any small provincial town in Normandy. Then came 7th June 1944, the day after the Allied Landings, when the town was liberated, having come through the fighting totally unscathed.

▲ *The fishmarket, headquarters of the tourist information centre.*

Modern Bayeux

THE BOTANICAL GARDENS

It was in the middle of last century that the botanical gardens were set up, under the impetus of Charlemagne Jean Delamarre (1772-1858), an engineer with a passionate love of plants. It lies on the Cherbourg road, on land purchased in 1856, and the layout was designed by the great landscape gardener, Eugène Bühler. The gardens were officially opened in 1864 and their lush greenery constitutes a haven of peace and tranquillity. In the centre is an extraordinary weeping beech with a trunk 40 metres - 130 ft. in diameter.

The Middle-Class 19th century Town

Industry underwent only a very modest expansion here, the main events in this respect being the building of the gasometer, the arrival of the porcelain works in 1812 and the arrival of the Paris-Cherbourg railway line at the end of the 1850's. Lace was to be one of the main success stories in the craftwork sector in Bayeux and the town now has a specialist school and an embroidery school.

The main period of urban development was over but there are a number of interesting buildings dating from this period i.e. the graceful Gothic-style Chapelle de la Miséricorde in Rue Général-de-Dais, the new cornmarket dating from 1830, the fishmarket built after 1845 (they are both in Rue Saint-Jean) and several buildings that are less impressive but more comfortable to live in than the ones constructed in the previous period. Most of them stand

▶ *The grain market (1830) used as a community and exhibition hall.*

along the main east-west thoroughfare which, in the town centre, consists of the Rue Saint-Jean, Rue Saint-Martin and Rue Saint-Patrice. At the end of this street, at the Vaucelles Roundabout, is the memorial to the liberation and, on the right, the botanical gardens.

Revival after 1944

In the months between the liberation of the town and the end of the Battle of France late in 1944, Bayeux was to see an enormous number of troops and equipment travel along the "by-pass" on their way to the front. The by-pass skirted the town and was the predecessor of the current ring road.

Peace returned and during the fifty years that have passed since then the town has developed still further aided by the increasing number of visitors, among them old soldiers and their families, and tourists from countries further and further afield who come to visit the Landing Beaches and the scenes of the main events in the Battle of Normandy. Bayeux' expansion has also benefitted from the rise of new sectors of activity. An industrial estate has been set up beyond the station, and a major bank has opened its national stocks

▲ *The Liberation Memorial at the Vaucelles Roundabout at the start of the Cherbourg road.*

BAYEUX, THE FIRST TOWN IN FRANCE TO BE LIBERATED

On 7th June 1944, British troops, greeted by enthusiastic crowds of local people, entered Bayeux without firing a shot and the town miraculously escaped damage. On 14th June, just one week later, Bayeux was in turmoil as it gave General de Gaulle a triumphant welcome. In his honour, the Landing Committee officially opened *the Mémorial De Gaulle* on 16th June 1990 in the rooms of the Governor's House in Rue Bourbesneur. A majestic bust of the General can be seen in the main courtyard. The Memorial contains numerous documents concerning the General's life during the days of the Free French Forces and the liberation of Bayeux. On the western exit from the town, at the Vaucelles Roundabout, there is the Liberation Memorial, the setting for official ceremonies involving heads of State, heads of government and high-ranking dignitaries from France and Allied countries.

◄ *14th June 1944. An ecstatic crowd throngs General de Gaulle on Place du Château, the square that was then renamed after him.*

▲ *Flanked by his companions, the General addresses the population on Place du Château.*

▼ *The Liberation Memorial at the Vaucelles Roundabout at the start of the Cherbourg road.*

and shares management centre on the outskirts of the town. Residential districts have sprung up in the suburbs.

Enormous efforts have been made as regards education. The town now has several large secondary schools, two lace making schools, a music school and an art school. Sports are well catered for in a number of high-quality amenities such as stadiums, a swimming pool and a multi-purpose sports complex.

BATTLE OF NORMANDY MEMORIAL MUSEUM

▲ *A general view from Boulevard Fabian-Ware. To the right is one of the American Army's Sherman tanks.*

The *Musée mémorial de la Bataille de Normandie* was opened to the public on 14th July 1981. It stands on Boulevard Fabian-Ware near the British war cemetery and it recounts the events of the summer of 1944, with descriptions of the people who took part, their equipment and kit. A great deal of space is also given over to contemporary documents (military papers, Allied and enemy press, photos of the battle etc.).

The museum is divided into (1) the Overlord Room which is subdivided into two areas (British and American) tracing the stages in the battle in chronological order; (2) the Eisenhower Room containing panels describing the efforts made by the Allies, the Free French and the Resistance, as well as artillery and engineering equipment and armoured vehicles. A large adjacent room is used for a range of different exhibitions. Since the ceremonies marking the fiftieth anniversary of the Landings, the room has been given over to an exhibition about the R.A.F.

◀ *The Overlord Room. A British officer from the 6th Airborne Division who parachuted into Ranville on 6th June 1944. Beside him is one of the 170 French soldiers in Commando no. 4 led by Commandant Kiefer, who landed at Riva-Bella. At the back is a Scottish officer.*

▶ *Detail of the cathedral façade.*

A Town of Artistic and Architectural Interest

The Bayeux of today is famous for its artistic and historic heritage and this constitutes its main attraction. First and foremost, there is "Queen Matilda's" Tapestry which is displayed in the Centre Guillaume-le-Conquérant (formerly the Grand Seminary), attracting some 500,000 visitors every year among them members of the British or Scandinavian royal families. Then there is the Battle of Normandy Memorial Museum which gives a greater understanding of the conditions under which the battle took place in 1944 and the various stages in it. The De Gaulle Memorial in the beautiful former Governor's Residence in Rue

◀ *"Healing Saint".*

▲ *A ceremonial landau being driven through a street in the urban district covered by a preservation order where it adds to the realism of a setting steeped in memories of times past.*

Bourbesneur contains a collection of documents and photographs dating from the days of free France and the Liberation, in honour of the General. A few yards away, on the square that bears his name, there is a monument commemorating his arrival in Bayeux in June 1944.

Close by is Rue des Chanoines, the birthplace of archaeologist Arcisse de Caumont in 1802. It leads to the cathedral, a masterpiece of the Romanesque and Gothic styles of religious architecture as practised in Normandy.

After leaving the great church, though, no visit would be complete without a stroll through the old streets with picturesque names such as Rue des Cuisiniers (Cooks Street), des Teinturiers (Dyers), des Chanoines (Canons), and Franche (free) said to have acquired its name because criminals were not taken along it. There is also Rue Quincangrogne whose name was aimed at people instigating legal action; they were requested to bow to the decision of the Court. These streets, like the ones in the town centre covered by a preservation order, are lined with old houses and the magnificent private mansions that recall the days of the monarchy. They go together to make up a unique backcloth which gives visitors the unexpected and delightful impression of having stepped back in time, whether or not the weather is fine, and whether or not they are seen in the evenings under the soft lighting from the old-fashioned street lamps.

BARON-GÉRARD MUSEUM AND DIOCESAN MUSEUM

Founded in 1900 thanks to a bequest from the family of Baron Gérard (1770-1836), one of David's pupils, the museum is housed in some of the rooms of the former Bishop's Palace on Place de la Liberté in the shade of the plane tree planted in 1797. There are three types of collection that are particularly outstanding i.e. the masterpieces of lace produced in Bayeux and in its vicinity, the porcelain produced between 1812 and 1951 when the factory was finally closed down after having been managed successively by the Langlois, Gosse and Morlent families, and finally the art collection ranging from Flemish Primitives to Impressionists such as Boudin, Caillebotte and Cross, and including works by Philippe de Champaigne, Boucher, Gros and Baron Gérard himself. There are also Aubusson tapestries, pieces of period furniture and two magnificent tombs with recumbent figures.

On the south side of the cathedral is the Diocesan Museum of Religious Art (*musée diocésain d'Art religieux*) which contains collections of vestments and church plate dating from the 17th, 18th and 19th centuries. There are also portraits of the bishops of Bayeux.

▲ *The Deanery chapel altar.*

▶ *A masterpiece of Bayeux lace.*

▼ *The tomb of Jacques André de Sainte-Croix, Lord of Ryes, 1628 (carved by Jacques Lefaye, a sculptor in Caen).*

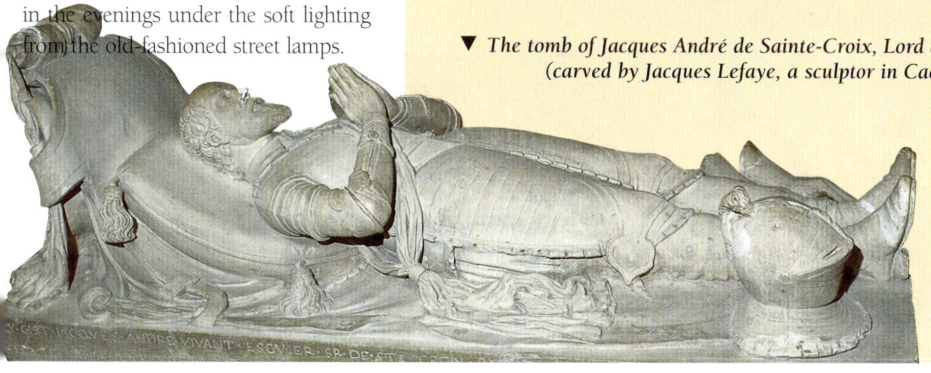

THE TAPESTRY CENTRE GUILLAUME-LE-CONQUÉRANT

The "tapestry" is actually a piece of embroidery almost 70 metres - 228 ft. long and 50 cm - 18 ins. high. It consists of eight lengths of linen embroidered with dyed woollen threads and includes 58 scenes. The first ones depict the preparation for the conquest of England by Duke William of Normandy, after Harold, his distant cousin, had committed perjury by reneguing on his promise not to seek the crown of England after the death of Edward the Confessor. Then comes a description of the work to prepare the invasion fleet and, finally, the Battle of Hastings in 1066 at which Harold was killed and victory was won by the Normans and their duke. He was crowned King of England on Christmas Day that same year.

It is thought that the embroidery, which is known as Queen Matilda's Tapestry or, alternatively, as the "Tale of the Conquest", was made at the request of Odo de Conteville, the Duke's half-brother. It is said to have been displayed for the first time on 14th July 1077 in the nave of Bayeux Cathedral, on the occasion of the consecration service.

It suffered during the French Revolution and again during the German Occupation but was then placed on show in the Deanery before being transferred to the William the Conqueror Centre in 1983 where almost half-a-million vistors file past it in admiration every year.

All photos : Bayeux Tapestry, 11th century, with special authorisation from the city of Bayeux.

▲ *Here, Duke William of Normandy crosses the sea on a large vessel and lands at Pevensey.*

◀ *William and Odo.*

▲ *A gracious young woman under a portico receives a light slap in the face from a tonsured cleric. This gesture is confirmation of a betrothal.*

◀ *At dawn on 14th October 1066, King Harold massed his troops on Senlac hill. Taking up a square formation and protected by shields, the Saxon infantry suffers a violent attack from the Norman cavalry. Bodies litter the battle field and are symbolically represented by the lower border.*

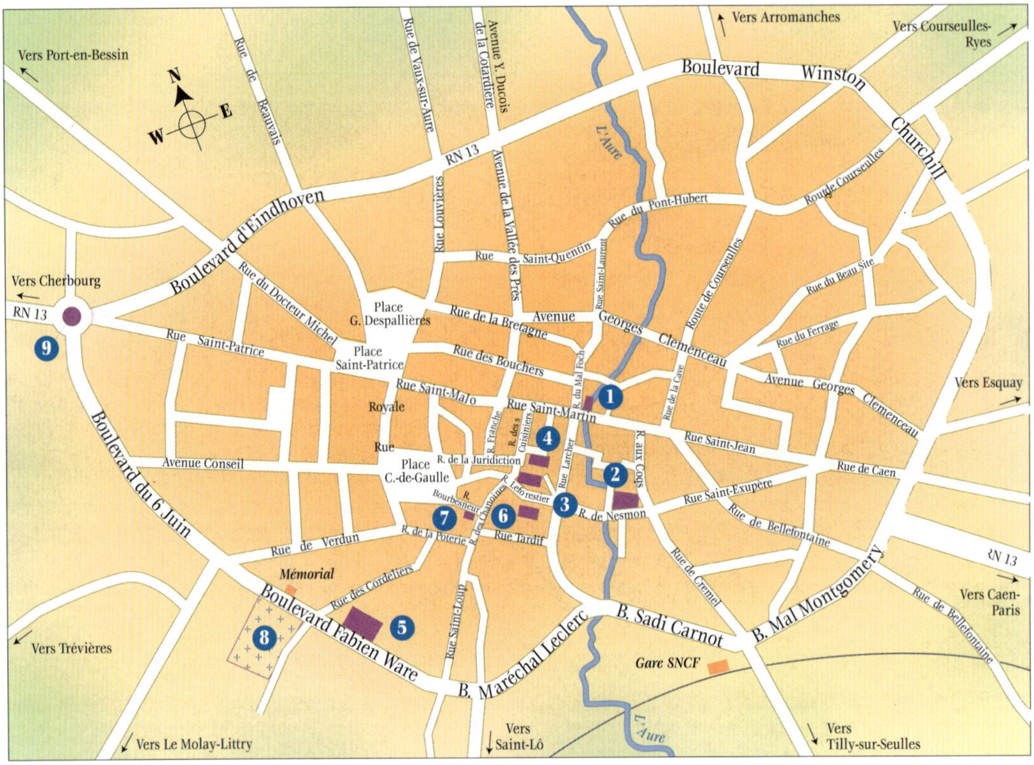

❶ Office de tourisme (Tourist Office)
Pont Saint-Jean
Tel. (33) 02 31 92 16 26

❷ Centre Guillaume-le-Conquérant: Bayeux Tapestry
Tel. (33) 02 31 92 05 48
Open daily. Signposted tour with audiovisual presentation and film. Last admission one hour before closing time.

❸ Cathédrale Notre-Dame (cathedral)
Open daily. No visits during services. Floodlit exterior: every evening but times vary depending on the season.

❹ Musée Baron-Gérard (museum)
Place des Tribunaux
Tel. (33) 02 31 92 14 21
Open daily. Last admission half-an-hour before closing time.
Collection of Italian Primitives, porcelain and Bayeux lace

❺ Musée mémorial de la Bataille de Normandie 1944 (Battle of Normandy museum)
Boulevard Fabien Ware
Tel. (33) 02 31 92 93 41
Open daily. Last admission one hour before closing time.

❻ Musée diocésain d'Art religieux (museum of religious art)
6 Rue Lambert Leforestier
Tel. (33) 02 31 92 73 80
Open daily.
Vestments and Roman Catholic church plate (18th-19th centuries)

❻ Conservatoire de la Dentelle deBayeux (lace making academy)
Hôtel du Doyen, 6 Rue Lambert Leforestier - Tel. (33) 02 31 92 73 80
Open daily except Sundays outside summer season.
Exhibitions, special events, sale of lace and lace making equipment.

❼ Musée mémorial "Le Général de Gaulle et Bayeux" (museum)
10 Rue Bourbesneur
Tel. (33) 02 31 92 45 55

❽ British Commonwealth war graves and memorial
Boulevard Fabien Ware.
Open daily.

❾ Monument de la Libération (memorial) Rond-point de Vaucelles.

Front cover: *The cathedral chevet.*
Vignette : *Detail from the Bayeux Tapestry, 11th century, with special authorisation from the city of Bayeux; Adam and Eve house; The statue of Poppa in the centre of Place du Général-de-Gaulle.*
Back cover: *Façade of the Hôtel de Castelly.*

Photogravure : Nord Compo, Villeneuve d'Ascq - Carte et plan : P. Mérienne
Maquette : B. Racine - Mise en pages : Studio des Éditions Ouest-France

© 2002 Édilarge S.A. - Éditions Ouest-France, Rennes
Cet ouvrage a été achevé d'imprimer en France par TPI, Betton (35)
ISBN: 2.7373.1970.6 - N° d'éditeur : 3359.02.03.04.05 - Dépôt légal : février 2002